Striking Surface

Striking Surface

Poems

Jason Schneiderman

The Ashland Poetry Press
Ashland University
Ashland, Ohio 44805

Printed in the United States of America

ISBN: 978-0-912592-70-1

LCCN: 2010927719

Cover art is by Dannielle Tegeder, *Nocturnal System Drawing and Atomic Nightlight*, 2009. Gouache, ink, colored pencil, graphite and pastel on Fabriano Murillo paper. 55 x 79 in. (140 x 200 cm). Image courtesy of Priska C. Juschka Fine Art.

Front cover design by Claudia Carlson

Back cover design by Mardelle McFadden

Author photo © 2010 by Star Black

ACKNOWLEDGMENTS

Grateful acknowledgment is made to the following publications, in which these poems, some in earlier versions, have appeared:

American Poetry Review, "Billboard Reading: War Is Over / Billboard Reading: (If You Want It)," "Notes on Detention," "Probability," "The person you cannot love"
Columbia Poetry Review, "I Love You and All You Have Made"
Connotations, "Elegy VIII: Missing You"
Court Green, "One"
EOAGH, "Ars Poetica I," "Ars Poetica II"
Failbetter, "Hyacinthus II," "Stalinism II"
Forklift, Ohio, "The Book of the Boy"
Harvard Review, "Elegy III (The Kübler-Ross Joke)"
Lit, "Wester"
Memorious, "Elegy VI (Metaphors for Grief)," "Elegy VII (Last Moment)"
Mis Poesias, "First Mouse"
New England Review, "Symbolic"
Ninth Letter, "Adorable Wounds"
Poetry for the Masses, "The Children's Crusade III"
Poetry London, "Modernism-O," "Physics V: Theology"
Provincetown Arts, "Rabbi Ishmael ben Elisha I"
Spork, "Carmen Miranda"
Virginia Quarterly Review, "The Children's Crusade III"
Washington Square, "Rabbi Jochanan ben Zakkai"
Zeek, "Sailor at Nostrand and Bedford"

"I Love You and All You Have Made" was reprinted by *Poetry Daily* on June 7, 2008.

"The Children's Crusade III" was printed as a limited edition broadside for Ari Banias's Uncalled For Reading Series by Micah Slawinski Currier under a different title.

I owe a deep debt of gratitude to Wayne Koestenbaum and Tom Sleigh for helping this manuscript find its current shape. Richard Siken's comments were invaluable. Kathy Graber has been an inspiration. Elizabeth Scanlon, Marion Wrenn, and Kathy Volk-Miller have consistently sustained me with their friendship and their faith in my work. Hugh McGowan, friend of my heart, you remain my most valued "outside reader." Without Ada Limón, this book would still be titled *Hyacinthus II*, and without Jennifer Knox, I'd still be boring. Power of Three! No poet could ask for a more supportive father than David Schneiderman. Michael Broder makes my life possible. Always, I love you.

The Fine Arts Work Center in Provincetown and The Corporation of Yaddo generously provided me with residencies where many of these poems were written. They were also two places my mother loved.

CONTENTS

I

The Children's Crusade III

When we reached Genoa, and the sea did not
open, and we were offered homes or exile,
there was little choice. We had survived the hot
summer, the frozen Alps. This was another trial
in our service of God. We left behind the weak
and walked to Pisa. The coastline was bleak,
but we were sure the sea would open elsewhere,
though each day, less sure. It was clear
that God had abandoned Nicholas, so now
we had no leader. We had no homes. We had
to continue—even when we saw how bad
were the ships that Pisa offered. I sat on the prow
as we left port, Palestine far, but in God's grace.
Of ourselves and our boat remains no trace.

Billboard Reading: War is Over
Billboard Reading: (If You Want It)

Aeschylus reminds us
that Might and Violence
are never far apart.

They work together.

In this case   not to bind Prometheus,

                        but to make sure
                        Hephaestus does.

A good question is

                        What would you die for?

Another question is

                        What would you kill for?

Prometheus is willing to be punished.

He knew he would be punished,

                        but not how.

Kierkegaard says,

                        Only one man is saved.

Kierkegaard says,

                        Every man can be that man.

The Oceanides will not leave Prometheus,

even at the risk of being punished themselves.

They love his story,

     though they wish it were different.

Sartre says that given the choice between slavery and death

    the good man chooses death.

Of course, the dead man

    chooses nothing.

Io comes upon Prometheus and asks for her future.

    Prometheus fears to tell her
    of how long she will suffer.

    At the end of her suffering,
    she will bear his liberator.

    If Io despairs to the point of suicide,
    Prometheus will never leave his rock.

But the Oceanides insist.

    They beg her story as a favor.

    So he tells it.

The 1952 movie *High Noon* is not a Greek tragedy.

    There is no clear idea
    of fate or inevitability.

Grace Kelly's Quakerism is superficial and reactionary,
an attempt to avoid the world and its violence.

> She seems to have no clear idea
> of what it is her god demands.

If *High Noon* were a Greek tragedy,
there would be a character named Nonviolence.

He would be a messenger from the mighty father.

He would beg Grace Kelly to put down the gun.

He would kneel on the street and fill his hair with dirt.

He would keen and wail.

He would cry,

> *You think you have saved your love,*
> *but you have forsaken the source*
> *from which your love came.*
>
> *You are tainted,*
> *and your love will sour.*
>
> *The thoughts of the hell that awaits you*
> *will kill the love you now bear.*

The movie ends without prophecy.

The movie ends with no higher law
than human love and human justice.

The fragment we have of *Prometheus Bound*
ends before the eagle arrives.

The fragments we have of Aeschylus end
before Prometheus is rescued.

Nietzsche insists that for the Greeks

there was no suspension of disbelief.

They were in the presence of Prometheus.

They became the chorus of Oceanides.

Nietzsche insists

the audience is the chorus;

the chorus, the audience.

Perhaps this explains why I want to save Prometheus.

I want to save him from the rock and the eagle.

I owe it to him.

Every human does.

Here is the essence of tragedy:

We are weak in the face
of the inevitable.

We can be noble or brave,
but we are always weak.

There is no tragedy now

because we do not accept our weakness.

Grace Kelly picks up the gun because we want her to.

No one watching the movie could want anything else.

A human facing another human is in a fair fight.

A human facing a god is not.

The Aztecs thought that they had met their gods.

        And then they were killed.

        It was proof they were right
        to regard us as gods.

Zeus sends Hermes to demand from Prometheus
the name of the warrior who will depose him.

        Prometheus refuses.

        But the war will come,
        and he will be freed.

We want the war to come.

It's what will free Prometheus.

It goes without saying,

        War's not over.

Don't make me say,

        I don't want it.

Adorable Wounds

"approach Christ in a new way... not vaguely, but casting yourselves into His sacred broken Heart and his five adorable Wounds."
—Gerard Manley Hopkins. Letter to his father. October 16, 1866.

When his side opened up
like a tent,
it was a little tent
because he was man-sized,
and when the water
came out,
it was not much.

The tent held nothing
but the spear
that made it,
and that
only briefly.

The other wounds
held only nails.

Is it blasphemy
to be the nail,
the spear? To want
to be the nail,
the spear?

That there was a body
is the miracle. There is only
one passion,
one adoration,
one love.

Let me sleep
inside that tent.

Let me be that nail.

Sailor at Nostrand and Bedford

I.

If you think that what I want
is to touch that sailor, to pull
his liquid body from those
polyester pants, you'd be
wrong. Look at him, all amble
and shucks, his bright white
cap shading the acne scars
that linger on his barely post-
adolescent cheeks. Was there
a time that I wanted to touch
every beautiful man that lived
in this world? If there was,
it has passed. Now, I want none
of that moment where he
discovers what his body
can do—what it is his tongue
will fit, where it is he wants
a tongue. Does it mean that
I have left the world? I am
happy for him, for his beauty,
hopeful that he will know
what to do with it, that it will
get him what he wants before
it fades, that he will learn
how much the uniform
enhances it, how much
he can get. And from
whom. But not from me.
I'm happy for him abstractly,
the way I'm sad for orphans,
the way I hope everyone can

find a way in this world.
I have no desire
to learn his name, to learn
his body, to learn
his breathing or his breath.

II.

There was a sailor, once.

What we wanted

was the same,

and each other

was the last place

we'd looked.

Don't think

I always want

a better medication.

Don't think

I'll pay

the same price.

Susan Kohner (Douglas Sirk's *Imitation of Life*)

I.

If it's true that what it means to be black
is inextricably bound up with what it means
to be white, that whiteness is ultimately
a byproduct of the production of blackness,
then what should I have learned
about Sandra Dee and Lana Turner?

II.

I'm a bad person, always wanting
the expedient, the practical, the easy.

At the end of the movie,
when Sarah Jane comes home

for the funeral, and the flowers
are everywhere, and Mahalia Jackson

is in full voice, I want Sarah Jane
to go—to get back in her car,

to go be white. She fought so hard
for it. It seems like she ought

to get to keep it.

III.

Susan Kohner, the actress playing Sarah Jane,
was widely seen, after the success of the film,
as actually being a light-skinned black woman,
and had great difficulty getting roles, despite
the Oscar nomination that put her in competition
with Juanita Moore, the actress playing her mother.

The very structure of the film calls into question
the whiteness of her body—the body of Sarah Jane
and the body of Susan Kohner were, are, finally,
inextricable. The success of the film, paradoxically,
destroyed her career, stripping her of a whiteness
that, like Turner and Dee, she had taken for granted.

IV.

Death tricks you twice. First about yourself,
and then about others. When loved ones die,

the finality of their absence often imbues
them with an ineluctable, demanding presence.

Does Sarah Jane owe her dead mother
more than she owed her live mother?

Of course not—but she can't deny her dead
mother what she denied her live one.

Hyacinthus I

Did you see what it was?

> A bat?
> A pipe?

I couldn't see.

They hit me from behind.

> Ha ha.

> Apollo took me from behind,
> then they killed me from behind.

Different "behind."   Makes it funny, see?

Not funny.   I know.

But as a flower
everything is funny: puns
                              riddles
                              aphids
                              cancer

Apollo saw, I think.   I don't blame him.

                              For not helping.

They had weapons.

                              Or a weapon.

                              I didn't see.

I'm a flower.
I die and live.
I'm everywhere.

Arachne says hi and hi and hi.

I turn my face to her.　　　　All day long:
　　　　　　　　　　　　　　Arachne, bee, gardener.
　　　　　　　　　　　　　　Arachne, bee, gardener.
　　　　　　　　　　　　　　Arachne, bee, gardener.

Who are we fooling?

I'm just plain dead.

Stalinism I

Be neither at the head
nor tail.

Valedictorian is a
death sentence.

Similarly,
last in class.

Similarly,
janitor.

All
will sweep

in the far corners
of the earth.

Between
whomever

you stand,
you sweep.

You are dust.
You are the dust

that is soon
to be swept.

Rabbi Jochanan ben Zakkai
(in which he escapes to Babylon to begin writing the Talmud)

They were killing and killing and killing,
so I died as best I could, slept in a coffin
and escaped with the unchecked dead,
my books safely around me, adding some heft
to the light-boned cadaver I made of myself
until I was in Babylon, free of the killers
who were killing each other by then, and being
killed—but as long as my books were safe
and my tongue could speak, it spoke fire.

Oh, the killers are dying, dying, always dying,
but they are never all dead, never, and I keep
my coffin close, though one mustn't die too often.

Echo (Narcissus)

I had been there every night watching. Watching him lure another one, fresher, younger. For years, he took them into the forest. I grew fatter, older. I satisfied myself with watching. Then he began to fade. He turned so many shades of translucent he was almost gone. I was like his mirror. Even at the end, he came to the forest every night. With a cane, even, he came. When no one would touch him, still he came. When the only sound in the forest was his crying, I moved towards him. "No," he said. "No," I repeated.

Hyacinthus II

It's stupid,
the love of these gods

who can only show it
after you've died

or they've hounded you
half across the world.

Who wants
to be a flower?

Better that weeds
should mark my grave

than the stars
should hold my face.

The Book of the Boy

The boy asks, "Why was I made?"
and the answer comes: "Because we
wanted you," which puzzles the boy.

"But there was no me to want," the boy
protests, and the answer comes: "Well,
we wanted something like you." And the boy asks

"Would any small person have done?"
and the answer comes: "Any small person
we made. It was critical that we be the ones

who made it." The boy hesitates.
The answers are getting angry. At last:
"So I was interchangeable? Then?

Before I was made?" The answer comes:
"Yes. Then. And now. We had hoped
you would be more specific by now.

All these questions." The boy wants
to sleep. The answers are very angry.
He has other questions, but he knows better.

He can hide in dreams, and maybe
by morning, he'll be someone
specific and loved and necessary.

One

I am one son and no father.

I am two sons and no father.

I am three sons and no father.

I am the bird that flies

between one father and one son.

I am not the bird that flies

between one father and one son.

Today is Ararat.

Today the flood begins.

Ars Poetica I

What is it you want?

      I used to know.

Has it changed?

      No.

What is it you want?

      Love. To be loved.

Has it changed?

      Love? Yes. It has.

What is it you want?

      To be brilliant. Effortlessly brilliant.

Has it changed?

      I never got that.

What is it you want?

      To be charming. Handsome.

Has it changed?

      I never got that either.

What is it you want?

I ask myself that all the time.

Has it changed?

No.

Ars Poetica II

You want to know
if I understand,

believing as you do
that understanding

is forgiving,
though, if pressed,

you would say,

> *There's nothing to forgive.*
>
> *I didn't do anything wrong.*
>
> *If you really understood,*
>
> *you'd know that.*

But there are both for me now:
understanding and forgiving.

They feel
like fatigue.

I'm trying to say:
Forgiving is the end of love.

The end of hate.
The end of strong emotion.

A poem should be
an understanding.

A forgiving.
But not the end of love or hate.

Maybe this
isn't a poem.

You say I talk
too much.

You think I should be quiet.
Like the moon

or the grass.
You say:

> *Look at all the sense you keep*
>
> *trying to make.*
>
> *You should know better.*
>
> *That's why I did what you think*
>
> *I need to be forgiven for.*

Fair enough.

If understanding
was the wrong thing,

I asked
for the wrong thing.

It was what I wanted
when I asked.

II

Elegy I (Work)

Whatever dead is, you are, and how you must hate that,
busy fixer of problems, busy stitcher of crafts. Do you know
how much work your corpse makes, now that your body
is nothing you tend yourself? Whatever you there is now,
she hates this work I do, this sorting of closets, this giving
of clothes, this shuffling of photos and papers. O mother.
O distributor of guilt and comfort. O repository
of guilt and comfort. I, too, hate this work of your grave,
this work of your aftermath. Father cries himself to sleep—
that is, if he sleeps. You warned me never to write anything down.
Said, *Never write anything you don't want your father to find.*
Said, *I never write anything I don't want your father to find.*
So now the work is you, blank slate, writing you, lazy bones,
writing you, dead corpse, you.

Elegy II (Elizabeth Barrett Browning)

At the funeral, I think *I should stop this—I should open the casket and see if there's a mistake.* I'm not one for jumping in graves, but right now it's only decorum keeping me out of that hole. If you were here, you would say that lots of people feel this way at funerals, that if people didn't feel this way at funerals, there wouldn't be zombie movies, and that the point of art is to make us feel less alone. Still, at this moment, I believe that my belief in your death is what's making you dead. I believe that if I just do the right thing, you won't be dead anymore. It sucks how belief is persistent and stupid. Knowing doesn't help with the believing, though it does keep me from making a scene. I don't stop anything. I join the line. I shovel dirt on your coffin. This is the living kicking you out. The dead go under the ground, so stay there. When you finished *Pet Sematary*, it creeped you out so bad, you couldn't sleep with the book in the house. Maybe we should have buried you with something to read. But not Stephen King. Robert Service, maybe. Some Elizabeth Barrett Browning.

Elegy III (The Kübler-Ross Joke)

You taught me that I can't lie down on the floor,
though it's my favorite place to lie, and it turns out
you can, at the airport, when your mother's dead.

Your death is a kind of get-out-of-jail-free card,
a hall pass for whatever I want to do, and the plane
has been cancelled, your funeral is in twelve hours,

and I can lie down on this floor. It's firm and sturdy.
I've lain down on rotting floors in decaying buildings,
but the floors of American airports are as smooth

and as firm as cool bathroom tile in a hangover.
Michael asks if this is depression, mentioning
that he preferred denial, as he explains to the security

guard that my mother died, that we're waiting
for the plane to be rescheduled, and we're left alone.
Did you catch the Kübler-Ross joke? It never got funny.

We much prefer the Mary Tyler Moore joke. Likewise,
the Oscar Wilde joke is always funny. Ditto the
Mary Baker Eddy joke. But the Kübler-Ross joke was stale

before we started. Do you know that her last books
were proofs of the existence of an afterlife?
Just like Socrates. I haven't read them yet,

but I can't imagine that I'll agree. I'd talk to you
differently if you were here. I wouldn't be angry
or depressed. I wouldn't be bargaining or in denial.

See? I told you it never got funny.

Elegy IV (Tallis)

I don't tell Dad that you never finished cross-stitching
the tallis piece because you were punishing him.
You wouldn't tell him, so why should I? I finished
the curtains you were planning, though I didn't line them.
I passed on the unfinished quilts to your quilting friend,
but no way I'm going to cross-stitch, and besides,
that was what, four, five crafts ago? After stained glass
and decoupage, but before basket weaving, toll painting,
knitting, crochet, and quilting. That's the problem
with this family—we're just no good at punishing
each other—or rather, no one can ever get results.
Everyone wants everyone else to be different,
but we can't make it happen. When you told me that
you were putting this off out of anger, I asked if Dad knew
you were punishing him, and you said, *No,*
he just thinks I'm lazy. And I said, *How's*
that working out for you, and you said, *Just fine.*

Elegy V (The Community of Mourners)

I know so many people who've lost loved ones
under terrible circumstances, and they welcomed
me in a way I don't think I deserved. Everyone's
mother dies. Mine was in surgery, sedated, numbed.

I wish I could see the dead as completed instead
of stopped, that some monument in my head
would be erected to you, instead of these scraps
of uncatalogued memory. Mourning's a trap,

isn't it? A way to pretend that what you lost
was better than what you had, a form of mis-
remembrance and lies. Mom, listen, of all of us,

only you believed in heaven or god. You lost
your faith, but it came back. You could send
me a sign. Help me believe again. Mend me.

Elegy VI (Metaphors for Grief)

Kathy says grief is like not having your skin on,
but I didn't feel vulnerable at first, or angry,
and I didn't cry or smash plates, and everyone
was nice to me, forgave me my general distraction,
made fewer demands on me than usual. I couldn't
go to parties, though. More than three people
in a room and suddenly I couldn't handle it.
Also, I started doing weird math with everyone
whose age I know, like *that person has now lived
three years longer than my mother*, or *that person
has five years to go until he reaches the age of
my mother's death*. I kept my skin, but the world
had a new gravity, as if my mother were now
the center towards which everything pulled. I'd think,
why finish this if Mom won't see it, or *why
go to work if my mother is dead?* She had never
been the axis my world turned on, but suddenly
everything seemed to revolve around her. No.
Not an axis. A skewer. A spit.

Elegy VII (Last Moment)

In her last waking moments, she was crying,
humiliated. The nurses had fucked up the
"cleansing" drink, and she had to drink it twice,
the part she hated most from the previous
procedures. We joked on the phone about the name
of the drink: "Go lightly"—the unintended
Breakfast at Tiffany's reference, poor pretty
Audrey revived as a gritty killer laxative.
After the second dosing, the smell in the ward
was so bad they put her in a quarantine bathroom,
the kind with a reverse airflow. When someone
dies, I think it's normal to be angry, to find
something to be angry about. Well, this is it.
Where I put my anger. What I wish I could change.

Elegy VIII (Missing You)

I thought I'd find you here, that I'd finish these poems
and you would stand out as clear as the day. As bright
as the moon. I hate those poets who tell you that
they love, but never make clear whom they love.
My mother's eyes are nothing like the sun. How do I
miss my mother? Let me count the ways. So where
are you? I couldn't believe you let yourself
be filmed for the video they showed at your tribute,
and I wanted to tell everyone, *That's only her voice
when she's nervous. That's only her face when she
has to be on display and she doesn't like it.* But at least
you were there. Everyone knows you can't write
your way out of grief. Everyone knows that grief
never turns into anything but grief, and OK, I can grieve
you forever. But I wanted you here, in the middle
of my book. Not a complaint about what I lost
or what it feels like to lose it. But you. Your smile.
Your denim dress.

III

The Children's Crusade I

We left no trace. Like Hamlin.

Remember Hamlin?

God said,

> *The man you become will bear
> no trace of the boy.*

God said,

> *The corpse you become will bear
> no trace of the man.*

God said,

> *Go,*

and we went.

God said,

> *Die,*

and we did.

The Children's Crusade II

The body is a gate,
a test. The body
is the ironworker's toy
that makes you believe
that the two pieces
can never come apart,
until you see how they do.
And when you hold
each piece separate,
as though you were God,
you will know
which piece to bury.

Stalinism II

Lately, it seems as if all I do is watch shows
about people who discover that they live
in worlds full of great and unexpected evil
that they alone have been chosen to fight
and have been given super powers
with which to do it.

Their ambivalence about their power
is in inverse proportion to their growing
martial arts skills, and by the end,
what looked like a single fight against
a single assigned evil has managed to
extend itself across multiple seasons.

Some days I miss the didacticism of
old school sci-fi: the white on the left side
warnings against racism, the pig-faced
pleadings for diversity, the ape/man
kiss that Sammy Davis Junior could
praise, even after his tentative romance

with Kim Novak had been sidelined
by mob goons. Some days I want to see
the lame, limp-wristed girl fight between
Mrs. Voorhees and that one surviving girl
at the end of *Friday the 13th* where no one
can fly or do spin kicks or judo.

I know I'm weak; that I should look
away, but I can't, or don't want to.
I'm sure there's something I haven't
learned yet that I will, but who knows
how many seasons it will take
before I get everything right.

Pedophile

I mention the thirteen-year-old boy with a life sentence,
tried as an adult, and Kevin says, "If he's being tried as an adult,
I don't see why I can't have sex with him," and for a moment
I think Kevin means the actual person in question, that he somehow
knew this actual thirteen-year-old boy, and that their probable,
mutual, sexual activity had been stunted, that some embodied hand
of a statutory rape law had stayed his, before I realize
that this must be a hypothetical, that we're states away
from this condemned boy, but then I notice that Kevin is really angry,
and I'm not sure if it's over the life sentence, or the age of consent,
or the inconsistency in the law. "I mean," he continues,
"if killing someone is the kind of adult action that makes
you an adult, then what the hell is a blow job?" And even as
I'm contemplating that he's right—that it doesn't make sense
that a thirteen year old can become an adult through violence
but not through sex—even as I'm contemplating this,
I'm also wondering how I can get out of this conversation.
There'll be no more coffee dates to discuss Derrida,
at least not with Kevin.

Physics V: Theology

Between space exploration and string theory,
we were quite sure that heaven and hell
were just metaphors (if anything at all),
but after the discovery that we actually exist
in twelve dimensions, it's quite possible
that heaven and hell are dimensional shifts
allowed for by death, and that Socrates
was right about that everlasting essence part.

Of course, the discovery of parallel universes
(well, possibility) fills me with great concern
about what evil-Jason is doing over there,
with his eye-patch and mustache, and I've decided,
just now, to grow a mustache myself,
and force that bastard to shave his off.

Physics VI: Time Zones

Yesterday, my math was so bad,
I missed a plane out of
San Francisco, and all of a sudden,
my free trip started costing
a lot of money.

I had my time zones wrong,
and I thought that time ran
east-west, but it doesn't,
and I thought I would get back
hours I had to give up.

I have to be in New York today,
and I am, which is the gift
of night, those vague hours
when everyone more or less agrees
to sleep, and the red-eye

is kinder than I deserve.

Carmen Miranda

I'm not sure I should be writing
about Carmen Miranda, but if I don't
I'm not sure anyone will, and
shouldn't you at least get a poem
when you give it your all and then
collapse just off-stage? If she'd
collapsed just a minute earlier,
she would have died on the *Ed Sullivan
Show*, and everyone in America
would have seen her die, and
she'd be in this special category
of people who died on live television,
like Lee Harvey Oswald, or Jerome
Rodale, where no one had time
to censor it. My host family in Russia
thought I was silly for turning away
from the hand-held corpse shots
on the evening news, and I tried
to explain that, in America, we have
a little more decorum, and I tried
to tell them about how they airbrushed
Jayne Mansfield's head out of the
newspaper photos of her car
accident, but they thought I was
talking about censorship,
and recently I heard that it was
just her wig, not her head,
even though she was decapitated,
and really, how can I talk
about American decorum when
there are all those photos
of lynchings, where no one turns away,
and everyone wants to be seen

with a corpse, but then they want
to be on the other side of the camera,
to be seen, and that's different
from wanting to see, or wanting
not to see, and I don't want to see
them, or know that it's America,
as American as Carmen Miranda
became, with her appealingly exotic
fruit hats, and her appealingly exotic
accent, and that all-American death,
because she couldn't stop
dancing on live TV, except
to die, which she did.

Wester

We're leaving the subway and Karen says,
"We're going to 10th Avenue," and I say,
"So we'll be going wester?" and Karen says,
being all mean about it, "No, we're not
going 'wester' because 'wester' isn't a word,"
and I say, "Well it should be," and Bill says,
"'Wester' isn't a word because there's no
'westest.' Like if I were in China and you
were here, we'd both be west of each other,
and besides, west only exists on earth, like
astronauts are never west of the earth or
east of each other," and I say, "Yeah, but
when we get where we're going, we'll be
more west than we are now," and Karen says,
"Yeah," and Bill says, "Yeah," and I say,
"Wester."

Symbolic

Foolish, the literal. Foolish to say,

>"A flower is just a flower."

Foolish is the man

>who hates the symbol,

insists each flower

>be only a flower,

who insists each color

>be only the color

on the surface

>of each petal.

The worst pick-up line in the world is not,

>"Hey, baby, what's your sign?"

The worst pick-up line in the world is,

>"A flower is just a flower."

Rabbi Ishmael ben Elisha I
(in which he fails to reverse the decree)

We thought poverty would protect us,

        but it did not.

We thought suffering would weaken us,

        but it did not.

When the golden eagle sat on our temple,

        we did not value gold.

When the taxes were heavy,

        we had nothing to give.

When our king killed his wife,

        his children,

there was nothing it pained us

        to leave.

The Numbers Wait with God for Humans to Invent Them

Three said, "Let me go to them—
I'm a magic number.
I can teach them man and woman and baby,"
and God said,
"They don't know that yet."

Five said, "They need me:
I'm the fingers on their hand.
Look how much they lose without me,"
and God said, "Yes, they do need you,
but they aren't ready."

And God smiled, and tussled
Four's hair, and picked up Two
and kissed him on the cheek.
The smaller numbers were eager to get to Earth,
where they were sure they would be loved

away from this confining madhouse.
Some and None had already
gone to Earth, and God had told
Few and Many
that it was time.

The smaller numbers missed their friends
and were sure
that things were better on Earth,
even though they knew that the numbers
that scared them—

a Million and a Trillion and their sisters
dragging their enormous bodies,
the imaginary numbers
who screamed at night
the things they knew,

the limping fractions and ratios
wandering like disfigured veterans,
the shadowy gloom
of the negative digits whose faces
they knew as their own—

they knew that those numbers
would come to Earth, in time,
to join them,
and that once they had arrived
there would be no escaping them, ever.

Rabbi Ishmael ben Elisha II
(in which he refuses to invoke Jesus to heal his nephew)

What he
can do

is not
for us.

He will
(soon

enough)
be Rome.

We will
(soon

enough)
be scattered.

What we love
is here.

What comes,
comes.

Speak not
the name

that cheats
death,

though
tempted.

Death comes
for you.

He is
an angel.

Modernism-O

Baudelaire calls to tell me to get an iPod
into this poem. "And Jason," he adds,
"say that I'm texting you." Charlie, look,
I'm not going to lie. I don't *text*.

First Mouse

Each mouse
is the first mouse,

the same failure
to live clean-

ly, the same
reminder

that you cannot
pass this world

without the taint
of another's

filth, without
having to kill.

Each mouse,
the first.

Probability

And now the world cracks open, like an enormous egg,
but not really, ha ha, nothing really cracks the world open,
not even that meteor that killed the dinosaurs. The world
was fine, still there, even if not quite the world it had been
the day before. Like how Dresden was still there, but not
quite Dresden, or Hiroshima, how it was there, but not quite
Hiroshima. The statistical probability of being a dinosaur
at the moment that the meteor hit is impossible to calculate,
because you would have to know whether any given dinosaur
was as likely to be any other given dinosaur, or whether
any living thing is as likely to be any other living thing—
but no matter what, the chance was tiny. No matter how you do
the math, every single dinosaur was statistically safe from
meteors. But then again, here we are, you and me, as human
and furless as we might have hoped, tiny teeth, opposable
thumbs, and all the birds locked out of our safe, insured
houses.

Notes on Detention

I.

The interrogation manual tells you that rule breakers want to be caught because, if you believe this, you will be a better interrogator. The truth of the statement is less important than that you be a better interrogator.

II.

How many striking surfaces on the human hand?

    Six.

On the foot?

    Three.

What is the strongest striking surface on the human body?

    The elbow.

On a cat?

    The claw.

On a snake?

    The teeth.

III.

It was an army colonel who couldn't bear
to watch the mine-detonating robot work
anymore, its spidery legs reduced to one
as it dragged itself towards the last mine
that it would be able to set off. The colonel
declared the test inhumane and stopped it.
The robot's inventor was surprised, as this
is what the robot had been designed to do.
The robot had not been intended to survive
the test. Perhaps the robot stepped
through the same door into humanity
that every victim steps out of. Perhaps
we should find that door.

IV.

Guess what happens if you can't sleep?

No, seriously, guess.

The person you cannot love

is brushing his teeth somewhere
in a prison, the White House,
the servant quarters. The person
you cannot love is giving a concert
right now, where an agent will sign her
and soon an entire marketing machine
will click into place behind her
and you will hear her voice every day
for six months or more, but you
will not love her. The person
you cannot love is having a limb
amputated and talking to a doctor
and calling his friend to ask how
the amputation went, or what
the prognosis is. There are too many
people in this world to not love,
continents full of them, even though
you remain sure that every city
(hell, every street) has at least one
person you could love, and now
you're getting angry, saying
There are many many people I love,
everywhere, there's no one I can't
love—I'm a good Christian—I love
everyone, but, oh, is Truth at your door
now, with his printouts of personal
ads and newspaper articles about
world leaders, and photographs
of third world children with unhealed
harelips, and press packets for
tomorrow's stars, and soon you will
admit to how much you cannot love,
and how the world will never

get better, and you will say, *Truth,*
please, show me less of the world,
find me someone I can make happy.

                                        after Carl Dennis

I Love You and All You Have Made

For M.B. in Bed-Stuy

The flowers are shocking on our shell-shocked block,
where everything is your doing—the garden plot
you wrested from the concrete with jackhammers
and bordered with cinderblock, the soil you carted home
in the wheelbarrow, the bulbs I helped you pick,
the jasmine you ordered on-line, the rose bushes
you brought home on the bus. I've always marveled
at your passion for plants—the custom-made boxes
on Fifty-seventh Street, the hanging baskets on
South Portland, the way plants grow for you,
the way cuttings hang on for you, years at a time.

The only plant I ever did well with was a ficus tree
named Charlie, who would only grow in my room,
and I still believe it was because he loved me.
Some days, I flatter myself to think
that I'm one of your flowers. Some days,
I flatter myself to think I'm not.

The Richard Snyder Publication Series

This book is the thirteenth in a series honoring the memory of Richard Snyder (1925-1986), poet, fiction writer, playwright and longtime professor of English at Ashland University. Snyder served for fifteen years as English Department chair and was co-founder (in 1969) and co-editor of the Ashland Poetry Press. He was also co-founder of the Creative Writing major at the school, one of the first on the undergraduate level in the country. In selecting the manuscript for this book, the editors kept in mind Snyder's tenacious dedication to craftsmanship and thematic integrity.

Editor Deborah Fleming screened for the 2009 contest, and Elton Glaser judged.

Snyder Award Winners:
1997: Wendy Battin for *Little Apocalypse*
1998: David Ray for *Demons in the Diner*
1999: Philip Brady for *Weal*
2000: Jan Lee Ande for *Instructions for Walking on Water*
2001: Corrinne Clegg Hales for *Separate Escapes*
2002: Carol Barrett for *Calling in the Bones*
2003: Vern Rutsala for *The Moment's Equation*
2004: Christine Gelineau for *Remorseless Loyalty*
2005: Benjamin S. Grossberg for *Underwater Lengths in a Single Breath*
2006: Lorna Knowles Blake for *Permanent Address*
2007: Helen Pruitt Wallace for *Shimming the Glass House*
2008: Marc J. Sheehan for *Vengeful Hymns*
2009: Jason Schneiderman for *Striking Surface*